HOW TO LEARN COMPUTER

1ST Edition 2024

By Er. Munna Chaurasiya

Trainer of Software Engineering and Programming Languages in H.S. COMPUTER CENTER

Dedicated to My Father, Mother and lovely students for his love and support

Contents

FUNDAMENTAL COMPUTER 4
PAINT 7
NOTEPAD 11
DOS(DISK OPERATING SYSTEM) 14
WORDPAD 17
SHORTCUT KEYS 20
MICROSOFT WORD 23
POWERPOINT 32
IMPORTANT SHORTCUT KEYS 34
MICROSOFT EXCEL 36
MICROSOFT PUBLISHER 39
MICROSOFT ACCESS 41
MICROSOFT OUTLOOK 44
NETWORK 47
TYPES OF NETWORKS 47
NETWORK TOPOLOGIES 49
INTERNET 51
TIPS FOR USING THE INTERNET EFFECTIVELY AND SAFELY 53
MULTIPLE CHOICE QUESTION 55

FUNDAMENTAL COMPUTER

1. Introduction to Computers

- **Definition**: A computer is an electronic device that processes data, performs computations, and executes instructions to carry out tasks.
- **Components**: Hardware (physical parts), Software (programs and applications).

2. Hardware Components

- **Input Devices**: Keyboard, mouse, scanner.
- **Output Devices**: Monitor, printer, speakers.
- **Storage Devices**: Hard drives, SSDs, USB drives, CDs/DVDs.
- **Central Processing Unit (CPU)**: The brain of the computer, responsible for processing instructions.
- **Memory**: RAM (volatile, temporary storage) and ROM (non-volatile, permanent storage).

3. Software

- **System Software**: Operating Systems (Windows, macOS, Linux), utility programs.
- **Application Software**: Word processors, spreadsheets, web browsers, games.

4. Data Representation

- **Binary System**: Computers use binary (0s and 1s) to represent data.
- **Units of Data**: Bit, byte (8 bits), kilobyte (1024 bytes), megabyte, gigabyte, terabyte.

5. Operating System (OS)

- **Functions**: Manages hardware and software resources, provides user interface, executes and provides services for applications.
- **Types**: Single-user, multi-user, multitasking, real-time.

6. Networking

- **Definition**: Connecting two or more computers to share resources.
- **Types**: LAN (Local Area Network), WAN (Wide Area Network), MAN (Metropolitan Area Network), PAN (Personal Area Network).
- **Internet**: A global network connecting millions of private, public, academic, business, and government networks.

7. Programming Languages

- **High-Level Languages**: C++, Java, Python – easy for humans to understand.
- **Low-Level Languages**: Assembly language, machine code – closer to machine language.

8. Databases

- **Definition**: Organized collection of data.
- **Database Management System (DBMS)**: Software to manage databases (e.g., MySQL, PostgreSQL, Oracle).

9. Security

- **Threats**: Viruses, malware, phishing, hacking.
- **Protection**: Antivirus software, firewalls, encryption, secure passwords.

10. Cloud Computing

- **Definition**: Delivery of computing services (servers, storage, databases, networking, software) over the internet (the cloud).
- **Benefits**: Scalability, cost-efficiency, accessibility, backup and recovery.

11. Emerging Technologies

- **Artificial Intelligence (AI)**: Machine learning, natural language processing.
- **Internet of Things (IoT)**: Network of interconnected devices.
- **Blockchain**: Decentralized digital ledger technology.
- **Quantum Computing**: Advanced computing using quantum-mechanical phenomena.

PAINT

1. **Introduction**
   - **Definition**: Paint is a simple graphics editing program included with Microsoft Windows.
   - **Purpose**: Allows users to create, edit, and view images.

2. **Features**
   - **Drawing Tools**: Brushes, pencils, and shapes (rectangles, ellipses).
   - **Text Tool**: Add text to images with various fonts and sizes.
   - **Colors**: Color palette for choosing and customizing colors.
   - **Image Editing**: Crop, resize, rotate, and flip images.
   - **File Formats**: Supports common image formats like BMP, JPEG, PNG, and GIF.

3. **User Interface**
   - **Canvas**: The workspace where images are created and edited.
   - **Toolbar**: Contains tools and options for drawing and editing.
   - **Color Box**: Displays the current colors for drawing and background.

4. **Common Uses**
   - **Basic Image Editing**: Simple edits like cropping and resizing.
   - **Creating Diagrams**: Quick sketches and diagrams.
   - **Educational Purposes**: Teaching basic graphic design concepts.

1. File Menu

The File menu contains options related to file operations:

- **New**: Creates a new blank canvas.

- **Open**: Opens an existing image file.
- **Save**: Saves the current image.
- **Save As**: Saves the current image with a new name or format.
- **Print**: Provides options to print the image.
    - **Print**: Sends the image to the printer.
    - **Page Setup**: Adjusts page settings before printing.
    - **Print Preview**: Shows how the image will look when printed.
- **From Scanner or Camera**: Imports images directly from a scanner or camera.
- **Send in Email**: Opens the default email client to send the image.
- **Set as Desktop Background**: Sets the image as the desktop wallpaper.
    - **Fill**: Fills the desktop with the image.
    - **Tile**: Tiles the image across the desktop.
    - **Center**: Centers the image on the desktop.
- **Properties**: Displays properties of the image (dimensions, colors, etc.).
- **Exit**: Closes the Paint application.

2. Home Menu

The Home menu contains tools and options for editing images:

- **Clipboard**:
    - **Cut**: Removes the selected area and places it on the clipboard.
    - **Copy**: Copies the selected area to the clipboard.
    - **Paste**: Pastes the content from the clipboard.
    - **Paste From**: Pastes an image from a file.
- **Image**:
    - **Select**: Selects a rectangular area of the image.

- **Rectangular Selection**: Selects a rectangular region.
- **Free-form Selection**: Selects an irregular region.
- **Select All**: Selects the entire image.
- **Invert Selection**: Inverts the current selection.
- **Delete**: Deletes the selected area.
  - **Crop**: Crops the image to the selected area.
  - **Resize**: Changes the size of the image.
  - **Rotate**: Rotates or flips the image.
    - **Rotate Right 90**: Rotates the image 90 degrees to the right.
    - **Rotate Left 90**: Rotates the image 90 degrees to the left.
    - **Rotate 180**: Rotates the image 180 degrees.
    - **Flip Vertical**: Flips the image vertically.
    - **Flip Horizontal**: Flips the image horizontally.
- **Tools**:
  - **Pencil**: Draws free-form lines.
  - **Fill with Color**: Fills an area with a selected color.
  - **Text**: Inserts text into the image.
  - **Eraser**: Erases parts of the image.
  - **Color Picker**: Picks a color from the image.
  - **Magnifier**: Zooms in on the image.
- **Shapes**: Provides a variety of shapes to insert into the image.
- **Colors**: Contains the color palette and options to edit colors.

3. View Menu

The View menu includes options to adjust the view of the image:

- **Zoom**:
  - **Zoom In**: Zooms into the image.

- - Zoom Out: Zooms out of the image.
  - 100%: Displays the image at its actual size.
- Show or Hide:
  - Rulers: Shows or hides the rulers.
  - Gridlines: Shows or hides the gridlines.
  - Status Bar: Shows or hides the status bar.
- Full Screen: Toggles full screen mode.

NOTEPAD

1. **Introduction**
   - **Definition**: Notepad is a simple text editor included with Microsoft Windows.
   - **Purpose**: Used for creating and editing plain text files.

2. **Features**
   - **Basic Text Editing**: Write and edit plain text without formatting.
   - **Find and Replace**: Search for specific text and replace it.
   - **Word Wrap**: Automatically wraps text to fit the window width.
   - **Status Bar**: Displays line and column numbers.
   - **File Formats**: Saves files with .txt extension but can open various text-based files.

3. **User Interface**
   - **Editor Window**: The main area where text is written and edited.
   - **Menu Bar**: Contains options for file operations, editing, and formatting.

4. **Common Uses**
   - **Quick Notes**: Jot down quick notes and reminders.
   - **Coding**: Simple coding and script writing.
   - **Log Files**: Viewing and editing system and application log files.
   - **Data Processing**: Basic manipulation of text data.

1. File Menu

The File menu contains options related to file operations:

- **New**: Creates a new blank document.
    - **Shortcut Key**: `Ctrl + N`
- **Open**: Opens an existing text file.
    - **Shortcut Key**: `Ctrl + O`
- **Save**: Saves the current document.
    - **Shortcut Key**: `Ctrl + S`
- **Save As**: Saves the current document with a new name or location.
- **Page Setup**: Configures page settings for printing.
- **Print**: Prints the current document.
    - **Shortcut Key**: `Ctrl + P`
- **Exit**: Closes Notepad.
    - **Shortcut Key**: `Alt + F4`

2. Edit Menu

The Edit menu includes options for editing text:

- **Undo**: Reverts the last action.
    - **Shortcut Key**: `Ctrl + Z`
- **Cut**: Removes the selected text and places it on the clipboard.
    - **Shortcut Key**: `Ctrl + X`
- **Copy**: Copies the selected text to the clipboard.
    - **Shortcut Key**: `Ctrl + C`
- **Paste**: Pastes the content from the clipboard.
    - **Shortcut Key**: `Ctrl + V`
- **Delete**: Deletes the selected text.
    - **Shortcut Key**: `Del`
- **Find**: Searches for text within the document.

- o **Shortcut Key**: `Ctrl + F`
- **Find Next**: Finds the next occurrence of the search term.
  - o **Shortcut Key**: `F3`
- **Replace**: Replaces text within the document.
  - o **Shortcut Key**: `Ctrl + H`
- **Go To**: Navigates to a specific line number.
  - o **Shortcut Key**: `Ctrl + G`
- **Select All**: Selects all text in the document.
  - o **Shortcut Key**: `Ctrl + A`
- **Time/Date**: Inserts the current time and date.
  - o **Shortcut Key**: `F5`

3. Format Menu

The Format menu provides options to adjust the text formatting:

- **Word Wrap**: Toggles word wrapping, which ensures all text fits within the window without horizontal scrolling.
- **Font**: Opens a dialog to change the font, style, and size of the text.

4. View Menu

The View menu includes options to adjust the view of the Notepad interface:

- **Status Bar**: Toggles the status bar at the bottom of the window (only available when Word Wrap is disabled).

5. Help Menu

The Help menu offers access to Notepad's help resources:

- **View Help**: Opens the Notepad help documentation.

DOS(DISK OPERATING SYSTEM)

1. Introduction

- **Definition**: DOS is an acronym for Disk Operating System, a family of operating systems primarily for x86-based personal computers.
- **Historical Context**: Widely used in the 1980s and early 1990s before the invention of graphical operating systems like Windows.

2. Key Versions

- **MS-DOS**: Developed by Microsoft, it became the most popular version.
- **PC-DOS**: IBM's version of DOS, developed in collaboration with Microsoft.
- **Other Variants**: DR-DOS, Free DOS.

3. User Interface

- **Command Line Interface (CLI)**: Users interact with the system through text-based commands.
- **Prompt**: Typically displays as C:\> indicating prompt to accept commands.

4. Basic Commands

- **File Operations**:
    - DIR: Lists files and directories.
    - COPY: Copies files from one location to another.
    - DEL: Deletes files.

- - REN: Renames files.
- **Directory Operations**:
  - CD: Changes the current directory.
  - MD: Creates a new directory.
  - RD: Removes a directory.
- **System Commands**:
  - FORMAT: Formats a disk.
  - CHKDSK: Checks the disk for errors.
  - DISKCOPY: Copies the entire disk.

5. Batch Files

- **Definition**: Text files containing a sequence of commands to be executed by the command interpreter.
- **Common File Extension**: .BAT
- **Usage**: Automating repetitive tasks.

6. Configuration Files

- **AUTOEXEC.BAT**: Executes commands at startup.
- **CONFIG.SYS**: Configures system settings and device drivers.

7. Limitations

- **Memory Management**: Limited to 640 KB of conventional memory.
- **Multitasking**: Lacks built-in multitasking capabilities, can run only one program at a time.
- **Graphical Interface**: Primarily text-based, with minimal support for graphical applications.

8. Legacy and Impact

- **Foundational Role**: Provided the groundwork for early personal computing and influenced the development of later operating systems.

WORDPAD

1. Introduction

- **Definition**: WordPad is a basic word processor included with Microsoft Windows.
- **Purpose**: Designed for creating and editing text documents with basic formatting.

2. Features

- **Text Formatting**: Allows formatting of text with different fonts, sizes, colors, and styles (bold, italic, underline).
- **Paragraph Formatting**: Supports alignment, indentation, and bullets/number lists.
- **Insert Options**: Can insert pictures, objects, and hyperlinks into documents.
- **File Formats**: Can open and save documents in multiple formats, including .rtf (Rich Text Format), .txt (Plain Text), .docx (Word Document), and .odt (OpenDocument Text).
- **Clipboard Operations**: Supports cut, copy, and paste functions.

3. User Interface

- **Ribbon Interface**: Modern versions use a ribbon interface with tabs like Home, View, and Insert, providing easy access to various tools and options.
- **Editing Area**: The main workspace where text is entered and edited.
- **Status Bar**: Displays information about the document, such as page number and zoom level.

4. Basic Operations

- **Creating a Document**: Open WordPad and start typing; format text as needed using the toolbar.
- **Opening a Document**: Use the File menu to open existing documents in supported formats.
- **Saving a Document**: Use the File menu to save the document in the desired format.
- **Printing a Document**: Use the File menu to access print options.

5. Differences from Notepad and Microsoft Word

- **Compared to Notepad**: More advanced formatting options and ability to handle richer text and multimedia content.
- **Compared to Microsoft Word**: Lacks advanced features like templates, mail merge, advanced grammar checking, and extensive collaboration tools.

6. Common Uses

- **Basic Document Creation**: Letters, notes, simple reports.
- **Text Editing with Formatting**: Documents requiring basic text formatting and insertion of images or objects.
- **Educational Purposes**: Teaching basic word processing skills.

7. Advantages

- **Ease of Use**: Simple and user-friendly interface.
- **Pre-installed**: Comes pre-installed with Windows, making it readily available.

- **Lightweight**: Uses minimal system resources compared to more advanced word processors.

8. Limitations

- **Limited Features**: Lacks advanced word processing capabilities found in full-featured software like Microsoft Word.
- **Basic Formatting Only**: Suitable for simple documents but not for complex formatting or professional publishing.

SHORTCUT KEYS

1. General Shortcuts

- **Ctrl + C**: Copy selected item.
- **Ctrl + X**: Cut selected item.
- **Ctrl + V**: Paste copied/cut item.
- **Ctrl + Z**: Undo last action.
- **Ctrl + Y**: Redo last undone action.
- **Ctrl + A**: Select all items in a document or window.
- **Alt + Tab**: Switch between open applications.
- **Alt + F4**: Close the active window.
- **Windows Key + D**: Show or hide the desktop.

2. File Management

- **Ctrl + N**: Open a new window.
- **Ctrl + O**: Open a file.
- **Ctrl + S**: Save the current document.
- **Ctrl + P**: Print the current document.
- **Ctrl + Shift + N**: Create a new folder.
- **Delete**: Move selected item to Recycle Bin.
- **Shift + Delete**: Permanently delete the selected item.

3. Text Editing

- **Ctrl + B**: Bold selected text.
- **Ctrl + I**: Italicize selected text.
- **Ctrl + U**: Underline selected text.
- **Ctrl + E**: Center align text.
- **Ctrl + L**: Left align text.
- **Ctrl + R**: Right align text.
- **Ctrl + Home**: Go to the beginning of the document.
- **Ctrl + End**: Go to the end of the document.

4. Web Browsing (Common across browsers)

- **Ctrl + T**: Open a new tab.
- **Ctrl + W**: Close the current tab.
- **Ctrl + Shift + T**: Reopen the last closed tab.
- **Ctrl + L**: Highlight the address bar.
- **Ctrl + D**: Bookmark the current page.
- **Ctrl + F**: Find text on the current page.
- **Ctrl + Tab**: Switch to the next tab.
- **Ctrl + Shift + Tab**: Switch to the previous tab.

5. Windows System Shortcuts

- **Windows Key + E**: Open File Explorer.
- **Windows Key + L**: Lock the computer.
- **Windows Key + R**: Open the Run dialog box.
- **Windows Key + I**: Open Settings.
- **Windows Key + S**: Open Search.
- **Windows Key + X**: Open the Quick Link menu.
- **Windows Key + PrtScn**: Capture a screenshot and save it to the Screenshots folder.

6. Accessibility Shortcuts

- **Windows Key + U**: Open Ease of Access Center.
- **Windows Key + Plus (+)**: Zoom in using Magnifier.
- **Windows Key + Minus (-)**: Zoom out using Magnifier.
- **Windows Key + Esc**: Exit Magnifier.
- **Alt + Shift + PrtScn**: Toggle high contrast mode.
- **Alt + Shift + Num Lock**: Toggle Mouse Keys.

MICROSOFT WORD

1. Introduction

- **Definition**: Microsoft Word is a widely-used word processing software developed by Microsoft.
- **Purpose**: Designed for creating, editing, formatting, and printing text documents.

2. Features

- **Text Formatting**: Change font type, size, color, and style (bold, italic, underline).
- **Paragraph Formatting**: Alignment, indentation, line spacing, and bullet/number lists.
- **Styles and Themes**: Apply consistent formatting using predefined styles and document themes.
- **Templates**: Use pre-designed templates for resumes, letters, reports, and more.
- **Tables and Charts**: Insert and format tables, charts, and other graphical elements.
- **Images and Graphics**: Add and edit pictures, shapes, SmartArt, and icons.
- **Review Tools**: Spelling and grammar check, thesaurus, word count, and track changes.
- **Collaboration**: Comments, co-authoring, and sharing documents.

3. User Interface

- **Ribbon**: A toolbar with tabs (Home, Insert, Design, Layout, References, Mailings, Review, View) containing groups of related commands.
- **Document Area**: The workspace where text is entered and edited.
- **Status Bar**: Displays information about the document, such as page number, word count, and zoom level.

24

25

Welcome Screen

जब आप Microsoft Word 2010 को Open करेंगे तो इसका Home Screen पृष्ठ इस प्रकार से होगा

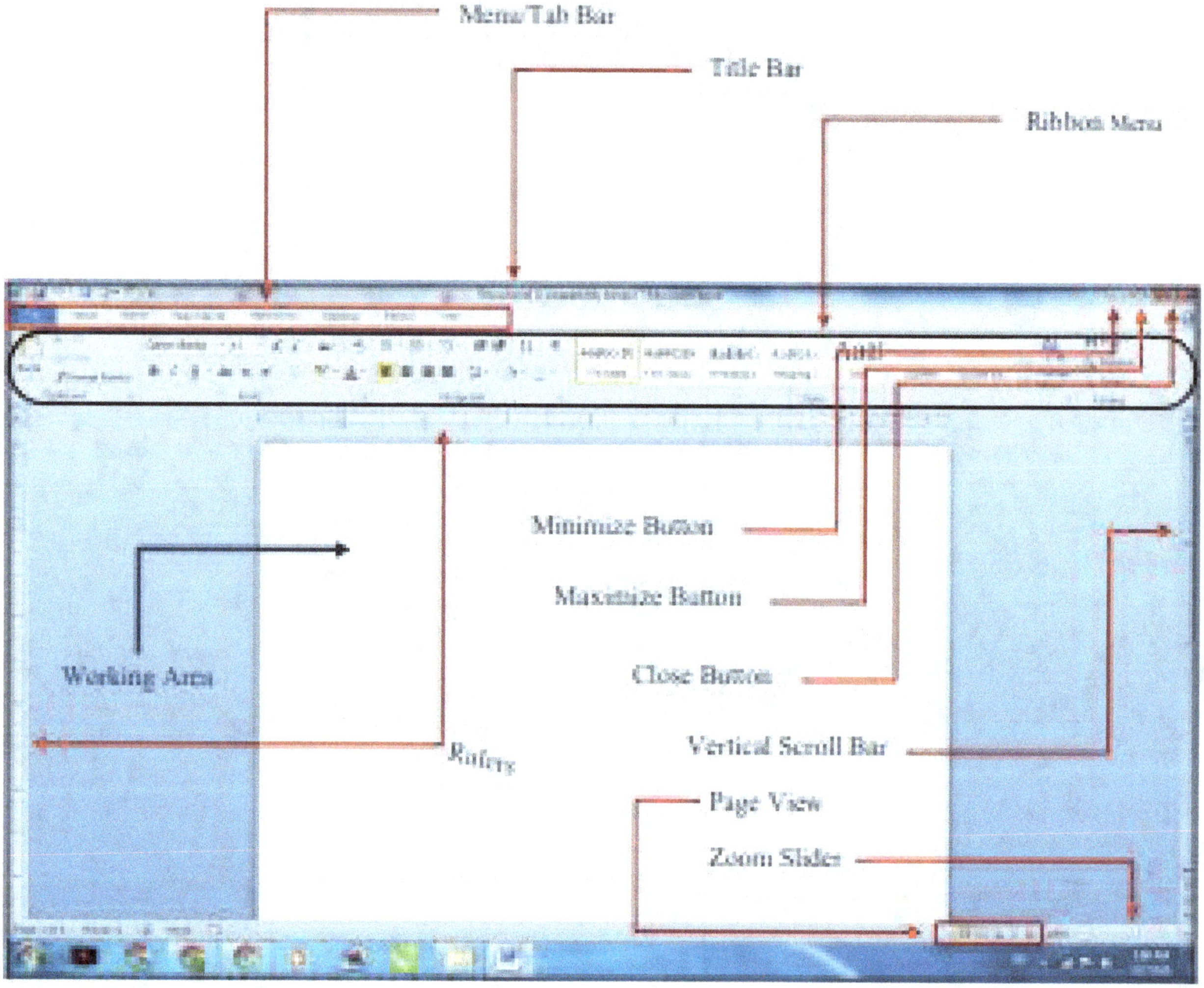

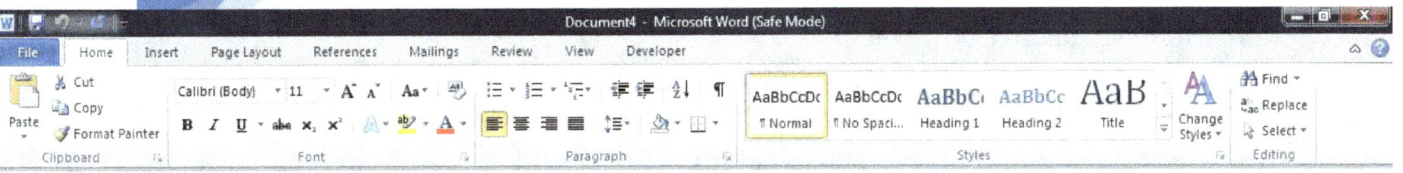

4. Basic Operations

- **Creating a Document**: Open Word, choose a blank document or a template, and start typing.
- **Opening a Document**: Use File > Open to open existing documents.
- **Saving a Document**: Use File > Save or Save As to save the document in various formats (.docx, .pdf, .rtf).
- **Printing a Document**: Use File > Print to access print settings and print the document.

1. File Menu

- **New**: Create a new document from a blank template or predefined templates.
- **Open**: Open existing documents.
- **Info**: View document properties, protect the document, and manage versions.
- **Save**: Save the current document.
- **Save As**: Save the document with a different name or format.
- **Print**: Access print settings, preview the document, and print.
- **Share**: Share the document via email or cloud services.
- **Export**: Create a PDF or other formats, change file type.
- **Close**: Close the current document.
- **Account**: Manage Microsoft account settings and Office updates.
- **Options**: Access Word options and settings.

2. Home Menu

- **Clipboard**: Cut, copy, paste, and format painter.
- **Font**: Change font type, size, color, style (bold, italic, underline), and effects (strikethrough, subscript, superscript).

- **Paragraph**: Align text, set line spacing, add bullets/numbering, increase/decrease indent.
- **Styles**: Apply predefined styles for headings, titles, and text.
- **Editing**: Find, replace, and select text.

3. Insert Menu

- **Pages**: Insert cover page, blank page, or page break.
- **Tables**: Insert and format tables.
- **Illustrations**: Add pictures, shapes, icons, 3D models, SmartArt, charts, and screenshots.
- **Links**: Insert hyperlinks, bookmarks, and cross-references.
- **Comments**: Add and manage comments.
- **Header & Footer**: Insert and edit headers, footers, and page numbers.
- **Text**: Add text boxes, WordArt, drop caps, and signature lines.
- **Symbols**: Insert equations and special symbols.

4. Design Menu

- **Document Formatting**: Apply themes, colors, fonts, and paragraph spacing.
- **Page Background**: Add watermarks, page colors, and page borders.

5. Layout Menu

- **Page Setup**: Set margins, orientation, size, columns, breaks, line numbers, and hyphenation.
- **Paragraph**: Adjust indentation and spacing.
- **Arrange**: Position, wrap text around objects, bring forward, send backward, align objects, group, and rotate objects.

6. References Menu

- **Table of Contents**: Insert and manage table of contents.
- **Footnotes**: Add and manage footnotes and endnotes.
- **Citations & Bibliography**: Insert citations, manage sources, and add bibliography.

- **Captions**: Insert and manage captions and create a table of figures.
- **Index**: Mark entries and insert an index.
- **Table of Authorities**: Mark citations and insert a table of authorities.

7. Mailings Menu

- **Create**: Create envelopes and labels.
- **Start Mail Merge**: Start a mail merge process.
- **Write & Insert Fields**: Insert merge fields, address block, and greeting line.
- **Preview Results**: Preview the merged documents.
- **Finish**: Complete the mail merge and print or email documents.

8. Review Menu

- **Proofing**: Check spelling and grammar, access thesaurus, and set language.
- **Speech**: Use the Read Aloud feature.
- **Accessibility**: Check document accessibility.
- **Comments**: Add, delete, and navigate comments.
- **Tracking**: Track changes, manage changes, and accept/reject changes.
- **Compare**: Compare and combine documents.
- **Protect**: Restrict editing and manage document protection.

9. View Menu

- **Views**: Switch between Read Mode, Print Layout, and Web Layout.
- **Show**: Show/hide ruler, gridlines, navigation pane.
- **Zoom**: Zoom in/out, view multiple pages, and open the Zoom dialog box.
- **Window**: New window, arrange all, split, view side by side, switch windows.
- **Macros**: Record, view, and manage macros.

5. Shortcut Keys

- **General Shortcuts**:

- **Ctrl + N**: Create a new document.
- **Ctrl + O**: Open an existing document.
- **Ctrl + S**: Save the current document.
- **Ctrl + P**: Open the Print dialog box.
- **Ctrl + W**: Close the current document.
- **Ctrl + Z**: Undo the last action.
- **Ctrl + Y**: Redo the last undone action.

- **Text Formatting Shortcuts**:
    - **Ctrl + B**: Bold selected text.
    - **Ctrl + I**: Italicize selected text.
    - **Ctrl + U**: Underline selected text.
    - **Ctrl + Shift + D**: Double underline text.
    - **Ctrl + Shift + K**: Format text as small caps.

- **Paragraph Formatting Shortcuts**:
    - **Ctrl + E**: Center align text.
    - **Ctrl + L**: Left align text.
    - **Ctrl + R**: Right align text.
    - **Ctrl + J**: Justify text.
    - **Ctrl + M**: Increase indent.
    - **Ctrl + Shift + M**: Decrease indent.
    - **Ctrl + T**: Create a hanging indent.
    - **Ctrl + Shift + T**: Reduce a hanging indent.

- **Navigation Shortcuts**:
    - **Ctrl + Home**: Move to the beginning of the document.
    - **Ctrl + End**: Move to the end of the document.
    - **Ctrl + Page Up**: Move to the previous page.
    - **Ctrl + Page Down**: Move to the next page.

- **Editing Shortcuts**:
    - **Ctrl + C**: Copy selected text or object.
    - **Ctrl + X**: Cut selected text or object.
    - **Ctrl + V**: Paste copied or cut text or object.
    - **Ctrl + F**: Open the Find dialog box.
    - **Ctrl + H**: Open the Replace dialog box.
    - **Ctrl + A**: Select all text in the document.

- **View Shortcuts**:

- **Ctrl + Alt + 1**: Apply Heading 1 style.
- **Ctrl + Alt + 2**: Apply Heading 2 style.
- **Ctrl + Alt + 3**: Apply Heading 3 style.
- **Alt + Ctrl + S**: Split the document window.

POWERPOINT

Key Features

- **Slides**: The basic unit of a PowerPoint presentation, where content is added.
- **Themes**: Pre-designed templates that provide a consistent look and feel across slides.
- **Transitions**: Animated effects that occur when moving from one slide to the next.
- **Animations**: Visual effects applied to objects on a slide (e.g., text, images).
- **Presenter View**: A special view that helps presenters see their notes and upcoming slides while presenting.

Basic Functions

1. **Creating a Presentation**
   - Open PowerPoint.
   - Select a template or a blank presentation.
   - Add slides using the "New Slide" button.

2. **Adding Content**
   - Text: Click inside text boxes to add content.
   - Images: Use the "Insert" tab to add pictures, shapes, icons, etc.
   - Charts and Tables: Also found in the "Insert" tab, these help visualize data.

3. **Formatting**
   - Themes: Found under the "Design" tab, apply a consistent design across all slides.
   - Backgrounds: Customize the slide background under "Design" -> "Format Background."

- Fonts and Colors: Adjust these in the "Home" tab to match the theme or brand guidelines.

4. **Adding Transitions and Animations**
   - Transitions: Apply transitions between slides using the "Transitions" tab.
   - Animations: Animate objects on a slide using the "Animations" tab.
   - Preview: Use the "Preview" button to see the effect.

5. **Setting Up a Slide Show**
   - From Beginning: Start the presentation from the first slide using the F5 key.
   - From Current Slide: Start from the current slide using Shift + F5.
   - Slide Show Options: Customize show settings under the "Slide Show" tab.

6. **Reviewing and Finalizing**
   - Spelling Check: Use F7 to check for spelling errors.
   - Comments: Add comments for review under the "Review" tab.
   - Rehearse Timings: Practice and record slide timings under "Slide Show" -> "Rehearse Timings."

7. **Presenting**
   - Presenter View: Use this view to see notes and upcoming slides (Alt + F5).
   - Navigation: Use arrow keys or a clicker to move between slides.

IMPORTANT SHORTCUT KEYS

File Menu

- **New**: Create a new presentation
  Shortcut: Ctrl + N
- **Open**: Open an existing presentation
  Shortcut: Ctrl + O
- **Save**: Save the current presentation
  Shortcut: Ctrl + S
- **Save As**: Save the presentation with a new name
  Shortcut: F12
- **Print**: Print the presentation
  Shortcut: Ctrl + P
- **Close**: Close the current presentation
  Shortcut: Ctrl + W
- **Exit**: Exit PowerPoint
  Shortcut: Alt + F4

Home Menu

- **New Slide**: Add a new slide
  Shortcut: Ctrl + M
- **Layout**: Change the layout of the selected slide
  Shortcut: Alt + H, L
- **Cut**: Remove the selected text or object
  Shortcut: Ctrl + X
- **Copy**: Copy the selected text or object
  Shortcut: Ctrl + C
- **Paste**: Paste the copied text or object
  Shortcut: Ctrl + V
- **Bold**: Make selected text bold
  Shortcut: Ctrl + B
- **Italic**: Italicize selected text
  Shortcut: Ctrl + I
- **Underline**: Underline selected text
  Shortcut: Ctrl + U
- **Find**: Find text in the presentation
  Shortcut: Ctrl + F

Insert Menu

- **Picture**: Insert a picture from file
  Shortcut: Alt + N, P
- **Chart**: Insert a chart
  Shortcut: Alt + N, C

- **Table**: Insert a table
  Shortcut: Alt + N, T
- **Text Box**: Insert a text box
  Shortcut: Alt + N, X
- **Header & Footer**: Add headers and footers
  Shortcut: Alt + N, H

Design Menu

- **Slide Size**: Change the size of the slides
  Shortcut: Alt + G, S
- **Format Background**: Change the background format
  Shortcut: Alt + G, B

Transitions Menu

- **Transition Effect**: Add transition effects between slides
  Shortcut: Alt + K

Animations Menu

- **Animation Pane**: Open the animation pane
  Shortcut: Alt + A, P
- **Add Animation**: Add an animation to a selected object
  Shortcut: Alt + A, A

Slide Show Menu

- **From Beginning**: Start the slideshow from the beginning
  Shortcut: F5
- **From Current Slide**: Start the slideshow from the current slide
  Shortcut: Shift + F5
- **Set Up Slide Show**: Set up the slideshow options
  Shortcut: Alt + S, U

Review Menu

- **Spelling**: Check spelling in the presentation
  Shortcut: F7
- **New Comment**: Add a new comment
  Shortcut: Alt + R, C

View Menu

- **Normal**: Switch to Normal view
  Shortcut: Alt + W, L
- **Slide Sorter**: Switch to Slide Sorter view
  Shortcut: Alt + W, I
- **Reading View**: Switch to Reading view
  Shortcut: Alt + W, D

MICROSOFT EXCEL

Key Features

- **Worksheets**: Individual sheets within a workbook where data is entered.
- **Cells**: The basic unit of a worksheet where data is entered; identified by a column letter and row number (e.g., A1).
- **Formulas**: Calculations performed using cell data (e.g., =SUM(A1)).
- **Functions**: Predefined formulas (e.g., =AVERAGE(B1)).
- **Charts**: Visual representations of data.
- **PivotTables**: Tools for summarizing and analyzing data.

Basic Functions

1. **Creating and Managing Workbooks**
    - Open Excel and create a new workbook (Ctrl + N).
    - Save workbooks using (Ctrl + S) or Save As (F12).
2. **Entering and Formatting Data**
    - Enter data into cells by clicking and typing.
    - Format cells using the "Home" tab (e.g., bold, italics, number format).
    - Adjust column width and row height by dragging the borders.
3. **Formulas and Functions**
    - Enter formulas starting with an equals sign (=).
    - Common functions include:
        - SUM: =SUM(A1

)

- AVERAGE: =AVERAGE(B1

)

- IF: =IF(C1>10, "Yes", "No")
- VLOOKUP: =VLOOKUP(D1, A1

, 2, FALSE)

4. **Data Analysis**
   - Sort and filter data using the "Data" tab.
   - Use conditional formatting to highlight data based on rules.
   - Create charts to visualize data (Insert tab -> Charts).

5. **PivotTables**
   - Create a PivotTable to summarize large data sets (Insert tab -> PivotTable).
   - Drag and drop fields to arrange data as needed.

6. **Data Visualization**
   - Use charts to represent data visually (Insert tab -> Charts).
   - Customize charts using the "Chart Tools" that appear when a chart is selected.

7. **Macros**
   - Automate repetitive tasks by recording macros (View tab -> Macros -> Record Macro).

8. **Protecting Data**
   - Protect worksheets and workbooks to prevent unauthorized changes (Review tab -> Protect Sheet/Protect Workbook).

Important Shortcut Keys

- **Ctrl + N**: New workbook
- **Ctrl + O**: Open workbook
- **Ctrl + S**: Save workbook
- **F12**: Save As
- **Ctrl + C**: Copy
- **Ctrl + X**: Cut
- **Ctrl + V**: Paste
- **Ctrl + Z**: Undo
- **Ctrl + Y**: Redo
- **Ctrl + F**: Find
- **Ctrl + H**: Replace
- **Ctrl + A**: Select all
- **Ctrl + B**: Bold
- **Ctrl + I**: Italic
- **Ctrl + U**: Underline
- **Ctrl + P**: Print
- **Ctrl + Shift + L**: Toggle filters
- **Alt + Enter**: Insert line break within a cell
- **F2**: Edit selected cell
- **F4**: Repeat last action
- **F7**: Spell check
- **Shift + F3**: Insert function
- **Ctrl + Arrow Keys**: Navigate to the edge of data regions

MICROSOFT PUBLISHER

Key Features

- **Templates**: Pre-designed layouts for various types of publications such as brochures, flyers, newsletters, and business cards.
- **Pages**: Individual sections or pages within a publication.
- **Text Boxes**: Areas where text is added, allowing for flexible placement and formatting.
- **Shapes and Images**: Tools to insert and manipulate shapes, pictures, and other graphic elements.
- **Design Checker**: Tool to check the publication for design inconsistencies or errors.

Basic Functions

1. **Creating a Publication**
    - Open Publisher and select a template or start a blank publication.
    - Choose the type of publication (e.g., brochure, newsletter) and customize the layout.

2. **Adding and Formatting Text**
    - Insert text boxes from the "Insert" tab and type or paste text.
    - Format text using options in the "Home" tab (e.g., font, size, color, alignment).

3. **Inserting and Managing Images**
    - Insert images using the "Insert" tab.
    - Resize and move images by clicking and dragging the corners.
    - Use picture tools to adjust image brightness, contrast, and crop.

4. **Working with Shapes and Designs**
    - Insert shapes from the "Insert" tab.

- Use the "Format" tab to customize shapes with colors, borders, and effects.
- Align and group objects for precise layout design.

5. **Using Templates and Design Elements**
    - Select from a variety of templates for different publication types.
    - Customize templates with your own text, images, and branding.
    - Apply color schemes and fonts from the "Page Design" tab to maintain a consistent look.

6. **Creating and Managing Pages**
    - Add new pages using the "Insert" tab.
    - Navigate between pages using the page navigation pane.
    - Use the "Master Page" feature to create consistent headers, footers, and design elements across all pages.

7. **Checking and Printing Publications**
    - Use the Design Checker to identify and fix design issues.
    - Preview your publication to see how it will look when printed.
    - Print the publication or save it as a PDF using the "File" tab.

Important Shortcut Keys

- **Ctrl + N**: New publication
- **Ctrl + O**: Open publication
- **Ctrl + S**: Save publication
- **F12**: Save As
- **Ctrl + P**: Print
- **Ctrl + C**: Copy
- **Ctrl + X**: Cut
- **Ctrl + V**: Paste
- **Ctrl + Z**: Undo
- **Ctrl + Y**: Redo
- **Ctrl + A**: Select all
- **Ctrl + B**: Bold text
- **Ctrl + I**: Italicize text
- **Ctrl + U**: Underline text
- **Ctrl + Shift + >**: Increase font size
- **Ctrl + Shift + <**: Decrease font size
- **Ctrl + K**: Insert hyperlink

- **Alt + F8**: Open the "Publisher Options" dialog box
- **Ctrl + Shift + L**: Insert a bulleted list

MICROSOFT ACCESS

Key Features

- **Tables**: Store data in rows and columns, similar to a spreadsheet but more powerful with relational capabilities.
- **Queries**: Extract and manipulate data from tables based on specific criteria.
- **Forms**: User-friendly interfaces for data entry and navigation.
- **Reports**: Format and present data from tables and queries for printing or viewing.
- **Relationships**: Define connections between tables to ensure data integrity and enable complex queries.
- **Macros**: Automate repetitive tasks and streamline database operations.
- **Modules**: Use VBA (Visual Basic for Applications) to write custom functions and advanced automation.

Basic Functions

1. **Creating a Database**
   - Open Access and create a new blank database or use a template.
   - Save the database with an appropriate name.

2. **Creating and Managing Tables**
   - Define tables by specifying fields (columns) and data types.
   - Set primary keys to uniquely identify each record.
   - Enter data directly into tables or import data from external sources (Excel, CSV).

3. **Using Queries**
   - Create queries to retrieve specific data from one or more tables.

- Use the Query Design View or SQL View to define query criteria.
- Perform calculations and data transformations within queries.

4. **Designing Forms**
    - Create forms to facilitate data entry and navigation.
    - Use the Form Wizard or Design View to customize form layouts.
    - Add controls such as text boxes, combo boxes, and buttons.

5. **Generating Reports**
    - Design reports to format and present data for printing or viewing.
    - Use the Report Wizard or Design View to customize report layouts.
    - Group and sort data within reports for better organization.

6. **Defining Relationships**
    - Establish relationships between tables to enforce referential integrity.
    - Use the Relationships window to drag and drop fields to create links.
    - Set relationship rules (e.g., Cascade Update/Delete) to maintain data consistency.

7. **Automating Tasks with Macros**
    - Create macros to automate common tasks and improve efficiency.
    - Use the Macro Builder to define actions and conditions.
    - Assign macros to form buttons, events, or database objects.

8. **Advanced Functions with VBA**
    - Write VBA code to create custom functions and procedures.
    - Access the VBA editor through the "Database Tools" tab.
    - Use VBA for advanced automation, data manipulation, and integration with other applications.

Important Shortcut Keys

- **Ctrl + N**: New database
- **Ctrl + O**: Open database
- **Ctrl + S**: Save database/object
- **F12**: Save As

- **Ctrl + C**: Copy
- **Ctrl + X**: Cut
- **Ctrl + V**: Paste
- **Ctrl + Z**: Undo
- **Ctrl + Y**: Redo
- **Ctrl + A**: Select all
- **Ctrl + F**: Find
- **Ctrl + H**: Replace
- **Ctrl + G**: Open the Immediate Window in VBA
- **F2**: Edit the current cell in a datasheet view
- **F4**: Toggle the Property Sheet
- **F5**: Refresh the active window
- **Shift + F2**: Zoom box for editing field contents
- **Alt + F8**: Open the Macro Builder
- **Alt + Enter**: Show the properties of the selected object

MICROSOFT OUTLOOK

Key Features

- **Email Management**: Send, receive, and organize emails.
- **Calendar**: Schedule appointments, meetings, and events.
- **Contacts**: Store and manage contact information.
- **Tasks**: Create and track tasks and to-do lists.
- **Notes**: Take and organize notes.
- **Folders**: Organize emails into custom folders.
- **Rules**: Automate email management through rules.
- **Search**: Quickly find emails, contacts, events, and tasks.

Basic Functions

1. **Email Management**
   - **Compose Email**: Create a new email using the "New Email" button or Ctrl + N.
   - **Reply/Forward**: Reply to or forward emails using the corresponding buttons or shortcut keys (Ctrl + R for reply, Ctrl + F for forward).
   - **Organize**: Move emails to folders, flag for follow-up, or categorize with colors.

2. **Calendar**
   - **Create Appointments**: Schedule events by clicking "New Appointment" or pressing Ctrl + Shift + A.
   - **Schedule Meetings**: Use the "New Meeting" button or Ctrl + Shift + Q to invite attendees.
   - **View Options**: Switch between day, week, and month views.

3. **Contacts**

- **Add Contacts**: Add new contacts using "New Contact" or Ctrl + Shift + C.
- **Groups**: Create contact groups for bulk emailing.

4. **Tasks**
   - **Create Tasks**: Add tasks using "New Task" or Ctrl + Shift + K.
   - **Track Progress**: Mark tasks as complete, set due dates, and prioritize.

5. **Notes**
   - **Create Notes**: Use "New Note" or Ctrl + Shift + N to jot down quick information.

6. **Folders**
   - **Create Folders**: Organize emails into custom folders.
   - **Rules**: Automate sorting of emails into folders based on criteria.

7. **Search**
   - **Instant Search**: Use the search bar to quickly find emails, contacts, calendar events, and tasks.
   - **Advanced Search**: Use advanced search features to refine search criteria.

Important Shortcut Keys

- **Ctrl + N**: New email
- **Ctrl + R**: Reply
- **Ctrl + F**: Forward
- **Ctrl + Shift + M**: New message
- **Ctrl + Shift + A**: New appointment
- **Ctrl + Shift + Q**: New meeting request
- **Ctrl + Shift + C**: New contact
- **Ctrl + Shift + K**: New task
- **Ctrl + Shift + N**: New note
- **Ctrl + 1**: Switch to Mail view
- **Ctrl + 2**: Switch to Calendar view
- **Ctrl + 3**: Switch to Contacts view
- **Ctrl + 4**: Switch to Tasks view
- **Ctrl + 5**: Switch to Notes view

- **Ctrl + E** or **F3**: Search
- **Alt + S**: Send email
- **Ctrl + Enter**: Send email
- **Ctrl + D**: Delete selected item
- **Ctrl + Shift + I**: Switch to Inbox
- **Ctrl + Shift + O**: Switch to Outbox
- **Ctrl + .**: Next message
- **Ctrl + ,**: Previous message

NETWORK

Key Concepts

- **Network**: A group of interconnected devices (computers, printers, servers) that share resources and communicate with each other.
- **Node**: Any device connected to a network (e.g., computer, printer, router).
- **Bandwidth**: The capacity of a network to transmit data, typically measured in bits per second (bps).
- **Latency**: The time it takes for data to travel from the source to the destination across a network.
- **Topology**: The physical or logical arrangement of network devices (e.g., star, mesh, bus).

TYPES OF NETWORKS

1. Local Area Network (LAN)

- **Description**: Connects devices within a small geographical area such as a home, office, or building.
- **Characteristics**: High data transfer rates, limited geographic range, often uses Ethernet or Wi-Fi.
- **Example**: Office network connecting computers, printers, and servers within a building.

2. Wide Area Network (WAN)

- **Description**: Connects devices over large geographical areas, such as cities, countries, or continents.
- **Characteristics**: Lower data transfer rates compared to LAN, uses technologies like MPLS, leased lines, or the Internet.

- **Example**: The Internet, a network connecting multiple LANs globally.

3. Metropolitan Area Network (MAN)

- **Description**: Covers a larger geographic area than a LAN but smaller than a WAN, typically a city or metropolitan area.
- **Characteristics**: Intermediate data transfer rates, often used by city governments and large organizations.
- **Example**: A city's public Wi-Fi network or a university campus network.

4. Personal Area Network (PAN)

- **Description**: Connects personal devices within a very short range, typically within a few meters.
- **Characteristics**: Very limited range, often uses Bluetooth or USB connections.
- **Example**: Bluetooth connections between a smartphone and wireless headphones.

5. Campus Area Network (CAN)

- **Description**: Connects multiple LANs within a limited geographic area, such as a university campus or industrial complex.
- **Characteristics**: Medium-sized network, usually owned and managed by a single organization.
- **Example**: University campus network connecting different buildings and departments.

6. Storage Area Network (SAN)

- **Description**: Specialized network that provides access to consolidated data storage.

- **Characteristics**: High-speed network, used for data storage and retrieval, often uses Fibre Channel or iSCSI protocols.
- **Example**: Network connecting servers to storage devices in a data center.

7. Virtual Private Network (VPN)

- **Description**: Provides a secure connection over a public network (usually the Internet) to connect remote users or sites.
- **Characteristics**: Uses encryption to secure data, allows access to a private network from remote locations.
- **Example**: Remote employees accessing their company's internal network securely over the Internet.

NETWORK TOPOLOGIES

1. Star Topology

- **Description**: All nodes are connected to a central hub or switch.
- **Advantages**: Easy to install and manage, failure of one node does not affect others.
- **Disadvantages**: Failure of the central hub can bring down the entire network.

2. Mesh Topology

- **Description**: Each node is connected to multiple other nodes.
- **Advantages**: High redundancy and reliability, failure of one node does not affect the network.
- **Disadvantages**: Expensive and complex to install and manage.

3. Bus Topology

- **Description**: All nodes share a common communication line (bus).

- **Advantages**: Simple and cost-effective for small networks.
- **Disadvantages**: Network performance degrades with more nodes, failure of the bus affects the entire network.

4. Ring Topology

- **Description**: Nodes are connected in a circular fashion, with each node connected to two others.
- **Advantages**: Data travels in one direction, reducing collisions.
- **Disadvantages**: Failure of one node can disrupt the entire network.

INTERNET

Key Concepts

- **Internet**: A global network of interconnected computers and servers that allows for the exchange of data and communication.
- **WWW (World Wide Web)**: A system of interlinked hypertext documents and multimedia accessed via the Internet.
- **IP Address**: A unique identifier assigned to each device connected to the Internet.
- **URL (Uniform Resource Locator)**: The address used to access resources on the Internet.
- **DNS (Domain Name System)**: The system that translates human-readable domain names (e.g., www.example.com) into IP addresses.
- **Gmail Storage** :- Gmail Storage is 15 GB

Components of the Internet

1. **Servers**
   - Host websites, applications, and data.
   - Provide services like email, file storage, and databases.

2. **Clients**
   - Devices like computers, smartphones, and tablets used to access Internet services.

3. **Routers and Switches**
   - Network devices that direct data traffic between different devices and networks.

4. **Internet Service Providers (ISPs)**
   - Companies that provide Internet access to individuals and organizations.

5. **Protocols**

- Rules and standards for communication over the Internet (e.g., HTTP, HTTPS, FTP, TCP/IP).

Basic Functions

1. **Web Browsing**
   - Accessing and navigating websites using web browsers (e.g., Chrome, Firefox, Safari).

2. **Email**
   - Sending and receiving electronic messages via email services (e.g., Gmail, Outlook).

3. **File Transfer**
   - Uploading and downloading files using FTP (File Transfer Protocol) or cloud storage services (e.g., Google Drive, Dropbox).

4. **Streaming**
   - Watching videos or listening to music in real-time via streaming services (e.g., YouTube, Netflix, Spotify).

5. **Social Networking**
   - Connecting and interacting with others on social media platforms (e.g., Facebook, Twitter, Instagram).

6. **Online Shopping**
   - Purchasing goods and services from e-commerce websites (e.g., Amazon, eBay).

7. **Search Engines**
   - Finding information on the Internet using search engines (e.g., Google, Bing).

Important Terms

- **Bandwidth**: The amount of data that can be transmitted over an Internet connection in a given amount of time.
- **Latency**: The delay between a user's action and the response from the Internet.
- **Cookies**: Small pieces of data stored on a user's device by websites to track and personalize user experience.
- **Firewall**: A security system that monitors and controls incoming and outgoing network traffic.
- **VPN (Virtual Private Network)**: A service that creates a secure, encrypted connection over the Internet to protect privacy.

TIPS FOR USING THE INTERNET EFFECTIVELY AND SAFELY

1. **Secure Your Connection**
    - Use strong passwords and two-factor authentication.
    - Keep your software and devices updated to protect against security vulnerabilities.
    - Use VPNs to secure your connection, especially on public Wi-Fi.

2. **Protect Personal Information**
    - Be cautious about sharing personal information online.
    - Use privacy settings on social media and other platforms to control who can see your information.

3. **Avoid Malicious Sites and Emails**
    - Be wary of phishing emails and suspicious links.
    - Use security software to protect against malware and viruses.

4. **Manage Online Presence**
    - Regularly review and update your online profiles and information.
    - Be mindful of the digital footprint you create with your online activities.

5. **Educate Yourself**

- Stay informed about the latest Internet trends, tools, and security practices.
- Be aware of the terms and conditions of the services you use.

Software	Run Command	Extension
PAINT	mspaint	.bmp
NOTEPAD	notepad	.txt
WORDPAD	wordpad	.rtf
DOS	cmd	------
MS WORD	winword	.docx
EXCEL	excel	.xls
POWER POINT	powerpnt	.pptx
MS ACCESS	msaccess	.accdb
MS PUBLISHER	mspub	.pub

MULTIPLE CHOICE QUESTION

- **Which of the following is the brain of the computer?**

  - A) Monitor
  - B) Central Processing Unit (CPU)
  - C) Keyboard
  - D) Mouse

Answer: B) Central Processing Unit (CPU)

- **Which of the following is a non-volatile memory?**

  - A) RAM
  - B) ROM
  - C) Cache
  - D) Register

Answer: B) ROM

- **Which part of the computer is responsible for executing instructions?**

  - A) Hard Drive
  - B) Memory
  - C) CPU
  - D) Monitor

Answer: C) CPU

- **What does RAM stand for?**

  - A) Random Access Memory
  - B) Read Access Memory
  - C) Read And Memorize
  - D) Random Allocate Memory

Answer: A) Random Access Memory

- **Which device is used to input data into a computer?**

- A) Printer
- B) Monitor
- C) Keyboard
- D) Hard Disk

Answer: C) Keyboard

- **What is the primary function of an operating system?**

  - A) To manage hardware resources
  - B) To create software applications
  - C) To perform calculations
  - D) To connect to the internet

Answer: A) To manage hardware resources

- **Which of the following is an example of application software?**

  - A) Windows 10
  - B) Microsoft Word
  - C) Linux
  - D) BIOS

Answer: B) Microsoft Word

- **Which of the following is the smallest unit of data in a computer?**

  - A) Bit
  - B) Byte
  - C) Kilobyte
  - D) Megabyte

Answer: A) Bit

- **What is the main purpose of a firewall in a computer network?**

  - A) To manage network traffic
  - B) To prevent unauthorized access
  - C) To store data

- D) To speed up network connections

Answer: B) To prevent unauthorized access

- Which of the following types of software is designed to help users perform specific tasks?

  - A) System software
  - B) Application software
  - C) Utility software
  - D) Middleware

Answer: B) Application software

- which tool in Microsoft Paint is used to draw free-form lines?
  - A) Fill with Color
  - B) Pencil
  - C) Eraser
  - D) Magnifier
  - **Answer:** B) Pencil
- What is the shortcut key to paste an image from the clipboard in Paint?
  - A) Ctrl + C
  - B) Ctrl + V
  - C) Ctrl + P
  - D) Ctrl + X
  - **Answer:** B) Ctrl + V
- Which of the following options in Paint is used to resize the image?
  - A) Crop
  - B) Rotate
  - C) Resize
  - D) Select
  - **Answer:** C) Resize
- In Paint, which tool is used to select an area of the image in an irregular shape?
  - A) Rectangular Selection
  - B) Free-form Selection
  - C) Select All

- D) Invert Selection
- **Answer:** B) Free-form Selection

- **What does the "Fill with Color" tool do in Microsoft Paint?**
    - A) It draws lines.
    - B) It fills an area with a selected color.
    - C) It erases parts of the image.
    - D) It zooms into the image.
    - **Answer:** B) Fill with Color

- **Which menu in Notepad contains the option to create a new document?**
    - A) Edit
    - B) File
    - C) Format
    - D) View
    - **Answer:** B) File

- **What is the shortcut key to save a document in Notepad?**
    - A) Ctrl + N
    - B) Ctrl + O
    - C) Ctrl + S
    - D) Ctrl + P
    - **Answer:** C) Ctrl + S

- **In Notepad, which option is used to search for specific text within the document?**
    - A) Go To
    - B) Replace
    - C) Find
    - D) Select All
    - **Answer:** C) Find

- **Which of the following options in Notepad inserts the current time and date into the document?**
    - A) F1
    - B) F3
    - C) F5
    - D) F7
    - **Answer:** C) F5

- **In Notepad, which menu contains the "Word Wrap" option?**

- A) File
- B) Edit
- C) Format
- D) View
- **Answer:** C) Format

- Which file formats can you save a document in WordPad?

  - A) .docx, .pdf, .rtf
  - B) .rtf, .txt, .docx
  - C) .rtf, .txt, .odt
  - D) .docx, .pdf, .odt

Answer: B) .rtf, .txt, .docx

- What is the shortcut key to create a new document in WordPad?

  - A) Ctrl + N
  - B) Ctrl + O
  - C) Ctrl + S
  - D) Ctrl + P

Answer: A) Ctrl + N

- Which tab in WordPad contains the options to change the font and font size?

  - A) Home
  - B) Insert
  - C) View
  - D) File

Answer: A) Home

- In WordPad, which feature allows you to add pictures to your document?

  - A) Insert Tab
  - B) Home Tab
  - C) View Tab
  - D) File Tab

Answer: A) Insert Tab

- **What is the purpose of the 'Word Wrap' feature in WordPad?**

    - A) To insert images
    - B) To wrap text to the next line within the window
    - C) To save the document
    - D) To print the document

Answer: B) To wrap text to the next line within the window

- **Which of the following options is available in the 'View' tab in WordPad?**

    - A) Zoom
    - B) Insert Picture
    - C) Font Size
    - D) Save As

Answer: A) Zoom

- **How can you access the 'Find' feature in WordPad?**

    - A) Press Ctrl + F
    - B) Press Ctrl + G
    - C) Press Ctrl + H
    - D) Press Ctrl + A

Answer: A) Press Ctrl + F

- **What is the function of the 'Paint Drawing' feature in WordPad?**

    - A) To add a new page to the document
    - B) To open a drawing canvas within WordPad
    - C) To print the document
    - D) To insert a table

Answer: B) To open a drawing canvas within WordPad

- **In WordPad, which command would you use to insert the current date and time?**

- A) Insert > Date and Time
- B) View > Date and Time
- C) Home > Date and Time
- D) File > Date and Time

Answer: A) Insert > Date and Time

- Which tab in WordPad allows you to change the orientation of the document (portrait or landscape)?

  - A) Home
  - B) Insert
  - C) View
  - D) Page Layout

Answer: D) Page Layout

- What does DOS stand for?

  - A) Disk Operating System
  - B) Digital Operating System
  - C) Disk On System
  - D) Data Operating System

Answer: A) Disk Operating System

- Which command is used to clear the screen in DOS?

  - A) CLS
  - B) CLEAR
  - C) ERASE
  - D) SCR

Answer: A) CLS

- Which command is used to display the version of DOS currently running?

  - A) VER

- B) VERSION
- C) DOSVER
- D) SYSVER

Answer: A) VER

- What is the command to change the current directory in DOS?

  - A) CHGDIR
  - B) CHDIR
  - C) CD
  - D) DIR

Answer: C) CD

- Which command is used to display a list of files and directories in DOS?

  - A) SHOW
  - B) LIST
  - C) FILES
  - D) DIR

Answer: D) DIR

- How do you create a new directory in DOS?

  - A) NEWDIR
  - B) MKDIR
  - C) CREATEDIR
  - D) DIRNEW

Answer: B) MKDIR

- Which command is used to delete a file in DOS?

  - A) ERASE
  - B) DELETE
  - C) REMOVE
  - D) DEL

Answer: D) DEL

- What is the purpose of the `COPY` command in DOS?

    - A) To copy files from one location to another
    - B) To delete files
    - C) To rename files
    - D) To display file contents

Answer: A) To copy files from one location to another

- Which command is used to rename a file in DOS?

    - A) REN
    - B) RENAME
    - C) NAME
    - D) CHGNAME

Answer: A) REN

- What does the `FORMAT` command do in DOS?

    - A) Displays the format of a file
    - B) Prepares a disk for use by erasing all data
    - C) Copies files from one disk to another
    - D) Displays the structure of the disk

Answer: B) Prepares a disk for use by erasing all data

- Which file contains the DOS system configuration commands?

    - A) CONFIG.SYS
    - B) AUTOEXEC.BAT
    - C) COMMAND.COM
    - D) SYSINFO.DOS

Answer: A) CONFIG.SYS

- What is the primary function of the `AUTOEXEC.BAT` file in DOS?

- A) To configure system settings
- B) To execute commands automatically at startup
- C) To display system information
- D) To manage disk partitions

Answer: B) To execute commands automatically at startup

- Which command is used to view the contents of a file in DOS?

  - A) TYPE
  - B) SHOW
  - C) VIEW
  - D) DISPLAY

Answer: A) TYPE

- What is the maximum filename length in DOS?

  - A) 8 characters
  - B) 16 characters
  - C) 32 characters
  - D) 64 characters

Answer: A) 8 characters (with a 3-character extension)

- Which command is used to display the current directory path in DOS?

  - A) PATH
  - B) SHOWDIR
  - C) PWD
  - D) CD

Answer: D) CD

- What is the default file extension for a document created in Microsoft Word 2016 and later?
    - A) .doc
    - B) .txt
    - C) .docx

- D) .pdf
- **Answer:** C) .docx
- **Which shortcut key is used to save a document in Microsoft Word?**
  - A) Ctrl + S
  - B) Ctrl + N
  - C) Ctrl + P
  - D) Ctrl + O
  - **Answer:** A) Ctrl + S
- **How can you insert a page break in a Word document?**
  - A) Press Ctrl + Enter
  - B) Press Alt + Enter
  - C) Press Shift + Enter
  - D) Press Ctrl + Shift
  - **Answer:** A) Press Ctrl + Enter
- **Which feature in Microsoft Word allows you to create a list with bullets or numbers?**
  - A) Font
  - B) Paragraph
  - C) Styles
  - D) List
  - **Answer:** D) List
- **What is the purpose of the 'Track Changes' feature in Word?**
  - A) To enable auto-saving of the document
  - B) To track the number of pages in the document
  - C) To track modifications made to the document
  - D) To track the number of words in the document
  - **Answer:** C) To track modifications made to the document
- **Which tab in Microsoft Word contains the 'Margins' option?**
  - A) Home
  - B) Insert
  - C) Page Layout
  - D) Review
  - **Answer:** C) Page Layout
- **What does the 'Ctrl + Z' shortcut do in Microsoft Word?**
  - A) Redo the last action
  - B) Undo the last action
  - C) Save the document

- D) Open a new document
- **Answer:** B) Undo the last action

• Which view allows you to see how your document will look when printed?
- A) Read Mode
- B) Print Layout
- C) Web Layout
- D) Outline
- **Answer:** B) Print Layout

• How do you create a hyperlink in a Word document?
- A) Press Ctrl + H
- B) Press Ctrl + K
- C) Press Ctrl + L
- D) Press Ctrl + J
- **Answer:** B) Press Ctrl + K

• Which option is used to change the orientation of a page to landscape in Word?
- A) File > Print
- B) Insert > Page Orientation
- C) Page Layout > Orientation > Landscape
- D) View > Orientation > Landscape
- **Answer:** C) Page Layout > Orientation > Landscape

• What is the shortcut key to select all content in a Word document?
- A) Ctrl + A
- B) Ctrl + C
- C) Ctrl + E
- D) Ctrl + S
- **Answer:** A) Ctrl + A

• Which feature in Word automatically moves text to the next line when it reaches the end of a margin?
- A) Word Wrap
- B) Text Wrap
- C) Line Break
- D) Text Break
- **Answer:** A) Word Wrap

• How can you insert a table into a Word document?
- A) Home > Table
- B) Insert > Table

- o C) Layout > Table
- o D) View > Table
- o **Answer:** B) Insert > Table

- Which command is used to check the spelling and grammar in a document?
    - o A) Review > Proofing
    - o B) File > Options
    - o C) Home > Editing
    - o D) Insert > Text
    - o **Answer:** A) Review > Proofing

- What does the 'Ctrl + B' shortcut do in Microsoft Word?
    - o A) It italicizes the selected text.
    - o B) It underlines the selected text.
    - o C) It bolds the selected text.
    - o D) It saves the document.
    - o **Answer:** C) It bolds the selected text.

- What is the default file extension for a presentation created in Microsoft PowerPoint 2016 and later?

- A) .ppt
- B) .pptx
- C) .pps
- D) .pdf

Answer: B) .pptx

- Which shortcut key is used to start the slideshow from the beginning in PowerPoint?

- A) F5
- B) F8
- C) Ctrl + S
- D) Shift + F5

Answer: A) F5

- Which tab in PowerPoint contains the option to add a new slide?

- A) Home
- B) Insert
- C) Design
- D) Slide Show

Answer: A) Home

- How can you insert a new slide in a PowerPoint presentation?

    - A) Press Ctrl + N
    - B) Press Ctrl + M
    - C) Press Ctrl + S
    - D) Press Ctrl + D

Answer: B) Press Ctrl + M

- What is the function of the 'Slide Sorter' view in PowerPoint?

    - A) To edit the content of the slides
    - B) To add animations to the slides
    - C) To rearrange the order of the slides
    - D) To add speaker notes

Answer: C) To rearrange the order of the slides

- Which feature in PowerPoint allows you to apply a consistent look to your presentation?

    - A) Slide Layout
    - B) Slide Design
    - C) Slide Theme
    - D) Slide Template

Answer: C) Slide Theme

- How can you add a transition to a slide in PowerPoint?

    - A) Home > Transitions
    - B) Insert > Transitions
    - C) Transitions > Transition to This Slide
    - D) Slide Show > Transition

Answer: C) Transitions > Transition to This Slide

- What does the 'Ctrl + K' shortcut do in PowerPoint?

    - A) It inserts a new slide.
    - B) It opens the hyperlink dialog box.
    - C) It saves the presentation.
    - D) It starts the slideshow.

Answer: B) It opens the hyperlink dialog box.

- **Which feature is used to add text to a specific area of a slide?**

    - A) Text Box
    - B) Word Art
    - C) Slide Layout
    - D) SmartArt

Answer: A) Text Box

- **What is the function of the 'Slide Master' in PowerPoint?**

    - A) To edit the content of individual slides
    - B) To apply animations to slides
    - C) To manage the overall design and layout of the slides
    - D) To add speaker notes

Answer: C) To manage the overall design and layout of the slides

- **How can you add speaker notes to your slides in PowerPoint?**

    - A) Home > Notes
    - B) Insert > Notes
    - C) View > Notes
    - D) Slide Show > Notes

Answer: C) View > Notes

- **Which view in PowerPoint is best for editing the content of individual slides?**

    - A) Slide Sorter View
    - B) Normal View
    - C) Reading View
    - D) Slide Show View

Answer: B) Normal View

- **How do you apply an animation to an object in PowerPoint?**

    - A) Design > Animations
    - B) Transitions > Animations
    - C) Animations > Add Animation
    - D) Slide Show > Add Animation

Answer: C) Animations > Add Animation

- **Which tab would you use to insert a chart into a PowerPoint slide?**

- A) Home
- B) Insert
- C) Design
- D) Slide Show

Answer: B) Insert

- What does the 'Ctrl + D' shortcut do in PowerPoint?

  - A) It duplicates the selected slide or object.
  - B) It deletes the selected slide or object.
  - C) It downloads the presentation.
  - D) It displays the slide in design mode.

Answer: A) It duplicates the selected slide or object.

- What is the default file extension for a presentation created in Microsoft PowerPoint 2016 and later?

  - A) .ppt
  - B) .pptx
  - C) .pps
  - D) .pdf

Answer: B) .pptx

- Which shortcut key is used to start the slideshow from the beginning in PowerPoint?

  - A) F5
  - B) F8
  - C) Ctrl + S
  - D) Shift + F5

Answer: A) F5

- Which tab in PowerPoint contains the option to add a new slide?

  - A) Home
  - B) Insert
  - C) Design
  - D) Slide Show

Answer: A) Home

- How can you insert a new slide in a PowerPoint presentation?

  - A) Press Ctrl + N

- B) Press Ctrl + M
- C) Press Ctrl + S
- D) Press Ctrl + D

Answer: B) Press Ctrl + M

- What is the function of the 'Slide Sorter' view in PowerPoint?

    - A) To edit the content of the slides
    - B) To add animations to the slides
    - C) To rearrange the order of the slides
    - D) To add speaker notes

Answer: C) To rearrange the order of the slides

- Which feature in PowerPoint allows you to apply a consistent look to your presentation?

    - A) Slide Layout
    - B) Slide Design
    - C) Slide Theme
    - D) Slide Template

Answer: C) Slide Theme

- How can you add a transition to a slide in PowerPoint?

    - A) Home > Transitions
    - B) Insert > Transitions
    - C) Transitions > Transition to This Slide
    - D) Slide Show > Transition

Answer: C) Transitions > Transition to This Slide

- What does the 'Ctrl + K' shortcut do in PowerPoint?

    - A) It inserts a new slide.
    - B) It opens the hyperlink dialog box.
    - C) It saves the presentation.
    - D) It starts the slideshow.

Answer: B) It opens the hyperlink dialog box.

- Which feature is used to add text to a specific area of a slide?

    - A) Text Box
    - B) Word Art
    - C) Slide Layout

- D) SmartArt

Answer: A) Text Box

- What is the function of the 'Slide Master' in PowerPoint?

  - A) To edit the content of individual slides
  - B) To apply animations to slides
  - C) To manage the overall design and layout of the slides
  - D) To add speaker notes

Answer: C) To manage the overall design and layout of the slides

- How can you add speaker notes to your slides in PowerPoint?

  - A) Home > Notes
  - B) Insert > Notes
  - C) View > Notes
  - D) Slide Show > Notes

Answer: C) View > Notes

- Which view in PowerPoint is best for editing the content of individual slides?

  - A) Slide Sorter View
  - B) Normal View
  - C) Reading View
  - D) Slide Show View

Answer: B) Normal View

- How do you apply an animation to an object in PowerPoint?

  - A) Design > Animations
  - B) Transitions > Animations
  - C) Animations > Add Animation
  - D) Slide Show > Add Animation

Answer: C) Animations > Add Animation

- Which tab would you use to insert a chart into a PowerPoint slide?

  - A) Home
  - B) Insert
  - C) Design
  - D) Slide Show

Answer: B) Insert

- **What does the 'Ctrl + D' shortcut do in PowerPoint?**

  - A) It duplicates the selected slide or object.
  - B) It deletes the selected slide or object.
  - C) It downloads the presentation.
  - D) It displays the slide in design mode.

Answer: A) It duplicates the selected slide or object.

- **What is the default file extension for an Excel workbook?**
    - A) .xls
    - B) .xlsx
    - C) .docx
    - D) .pptx
- **Which function is used to find the largest number in a range of numbers?**
    - A) MIN()
    - B) MAX()
    - C) LARGE()
    - D) GREATEST()
- **In Excel, what does the CONCATENATE function do?**
    - A) Adds numbers together
    - B) Joins two or more text strings into one string
    - C) Finds the average of a range of numbers
    - D) Counts the number of cells that meet a criterion
- **Which of the following is NOT an option in the "Paste Special" dialog box?**
    - A) Values
    - B) Formatting
    - C) Data Validation
    - D) Templates
- **How can you quickly adjust the width of a column to fit the content?**
    - A) Double-click the right border of the column header
    - B) Right-click the column header and select "AutoFit"
    - C) Go to the "File" menu and select "AutoFit"
    - D) Use the "Format Painter" tool
- **What symbol is used to start a formula in Excel?**
    - A) @
    - B) =
    - C) #
    - D) $
- **Which of the following Excel features allows you to visualize data trends over a series of values?**
    - A) PivotTable
    - B) Sparklines
    - C) Data Validation
    - D) Conditional Formatting

- **What does the VLOOKUP function do?**
    - A) Looks up a value in a vertical table
    - B) Looks up a value in a horizontal table
    - C) Looks up a value in a diagonal table
    - D) Looks up a value in a circular table
- **Which keyboard shortcut is used to save a workbook in Excel?**
    - A) Ctrl + S
    - B) Ctrl + A
    - C) Ctrl + P
    - D) Ctrl + F
- **What is the purpose of the Freeze Panes feature in Excel?**
    - A) To create a backup of the workbook
    - B) To prevent changes to the workbook
    - C) To keep rows and columns visible while scrolling through the worksheet
    - D) To lock the worksheet for editing
- **What is Microsoft Publisher primarily used for?**
    - A) Creating spreadsheets
    - B) Managing databases
    - C) Desktop publishing
    - D) Writing code
- **Which file extension is used by default for a Microsoft Publisher file?**
    - A) .pub
    - B) .docx
    - C) .pptx
    - D) .xlsx
- **In Publisher, what is a "Master Page"?**
    - A) A page template that can be applied to multiple pages
    - B) The first page of the document
    - C) The final page of the document
    - D) A page that cannot be edited
- **Which feature in Publisher allows you to align text and objects to specific locations?**
    - A) Gridlines
    - B) Paragraph formatting
    - C) Page setup
    - D) Style sheets
- **What is the purpose of the Design Checker in Publisher?**
    - A) To correct spelling errors
    - B) To check the document for design inconsistencies
    - C) To save the document in different formats
    - D) To adjust the document margins
- **Which of the following is NOT a type of object you can insert into a Publisher document?**
    - A) Text Box
    - B) Table
    - C) Chart
    - D) Code Snippet
- **How can you ensure that text within a text box in Publisher does not overflow?**

- o A) Adjust the font size
- o B) Use the "AutoFit Text" option
- o C) Increase the text box size
- o D) All of the above

- **Which of the following can be used to create a uniform look across multiple pages in a Publisher document?**
  - o A) Master Pages
  - o B) Gridlines
  - o C) Table of Contents
  - o D) Embedded Excel Sheets

- **What is the purpose of the "Mail Merge" feature in Publisher?**
  - o A) To send emails directly from Publisher
  - o B) To combine multiple Publisher files into one
  - o C) To create personalized publications for a list of recipients
  - o D) To merge different design elements into a single page

- **Which tool would you use to change the background color of a page in Publisher?**
  - o A) Page Color
  - o B) Background Fill
  - o C) Page Layout
  - o D) Color Picker

- **What is Microsoft Access primarily used for?**

  - A) Creating presentations
  - B) Managing databases
  - C) Editing photos
  - D) Writing code

- **Which file extension is used by default for a Microsoft Access database file?**

  - A) .accdb
  - B) .mdb
  - C) .xlsx
  - D) .dbf

- **In Access, what is a "primary key"?**

  - A) A unique identifier for each record in a table
  - B) A field that allows duplicate values
  - C) A type of query
  - D) A form control

- **Which of the following is NOT a type of object in Access?**

  - A) Table
  - B) Query
  - C) Worksheet

- D) Report

- **What does a "query" in Access do?**

  - A) Stores data
  - B) Retrieves specific data based on criteria
  - C) Formats data for printing
  - D) Creates data entry forms

- **What is the purpose of a "form" in Access?**

  - A) To organize data into rows and columns
  - B) To create a user-friendly interface for data entry
  - C) To generate printed reports
  - D) To define relationships between tables

- **Which of the following is used to create a relationship between two tables in Access?**

  - A) Data Type
  - B) Primary Key
  - C) Foreign Key
  - D) Validation Rule

- **In Access, what is a "report"?**

  - A) A summary of data formatted for printing
  - B) A tool for entering data
  - C) A tool for importing data
  - D) A type of query

- **Which view in Access allows you to design the structure of a table?**

  - A) Datasheet View
  - B) Design View
  - C) Layout View
  - D) Form View

- **What is the purpose of the "Lookup Wizard" in Access?**

  - A) To search for records in a table
  - B) To create a lookup field that allows the user to select a value from another table or list
  - C) To format data in a table
  - D) To create a new query

- **What does "HTTP" stand for?**

  - A) HyperText Transmission Protocol

- B) HyperText Transfer Protocol
- C) HyperText Transaction Protocol
- D) HyperText Transfer Procedure

- **Which of the following is a common web browser?**

  - A) Microsoft Word
  - B) Adobe Photoshop
  - C) Google Chrome
  - D) Excel

- **What is the primary function of a search engine?**

  - A) To display websites
  - B) To organize files on a computer
  - C) To index and retrieve information on the web
  - D) To edit text documents

- **What does "URL" stand for?**

  - A) Universal Resource Locator
  - B) Uniform Resource Locator
  - C) Universal Retrieval Locator
  - D) Uniform Retrieval Locator

- **Which protocol is used to send emails over the internet?**

  - A) FTP
  - B) HTTP
  - C) SMTP
  - D) IMAP

- **Which of the following is an example of a top-level domain (TLD)?**

  - A) .com
  - B) /index.html
  - C) www
  - D) http

- **What is a firewall used for?**

  - A) To manage email accounts
  - B) To protect a network from unauthorized access
  - C) To speed up internet connections
  - D) To store website data

- **What does "IP" stand for in the context of IP address?**

- A) Internet Provider
- B) Internet Protocol
- C) Internal Protocol
- D) Information Provider

- **Which of the following is an example of a social media platform?**

  - A) Microsoft Office
  - B) Linux
  - C) Facebook
  - D) Apache

- **What does "DNS" stand for?**

  - A) Domain Name System
  - B) Digital Network Service
  - C) Data Network Server
  - D) Domain Network Server

- **What is the primary purpose of a computer network?**

  - A) To perform calculations
  - B) To connect and share resources
  - C) To play games
  - D) To store data

- **What does "LAN" stand for?**

  - A) Large Area Network
  - B) Local Area Network
  - C) Linked Area Network
  - D) Limited Area Network

- **Which device is used to connect multiple computers within a local area network?**

  - A) Router
  - B) Modem
  - C) Switch
  - D) Firewall

- **What does "IP" in "IP address" stand for?**

  - A) Internet Protocol
  - B) Internal Program
  - C) Information Provider
  - D) Internet Provider

- Which of the following is a common protocol used for sending and receiving emails?

    - A) FTP
    - B) HTTP
    - C) SMTP
    - D) SNMP

- What does "VPN" stand for?

    - A) Virtual Private Network
    - B) Virtual Public Network
    - C) Variable Private Network
    - D) Verified Public Network

- Which layer of the OSI model is responsible for data encryption?

    - A) Physical layer
    - B) Data link layer
    - C) Network layer
    - D) Presentation layer

- What is the main function of a router in a network?

    - A) To connect devices within a local network
    - B) To forward data packets between different networks
    - C) To block unauthorized access
    - D) To provide power to network devices

- What does "DNS" stand for in networking?

    - A) Digital Network System
    - B) Data Network Server
    - C) Domain Name System
    - D) Domain Network Server

- Which protocol is used for secure communication over the internet?

    - A) FTP
    - B) SSH
    - C) Telnet
    - D) SMTP

- What type of service is Gmail?

    - A) Cloud storage
    - B) Email service
    - C) Instant messaging

- D) Social networking

- **Which company provides Gmail?**

  - A) Microsoft
  - B) Yahoo
  - C) Google
  - D) Apple

- **What is the maximum size of an email attachment you can send via Gmail?**

  - A) 10 MB
  - B) 25 MB
  - C) 50 MB
  - D) 100 MB

- **Which feature in Gmail allows you to organize your emails by applying labels?**

  - A) Folders
  - B) Filters
  - C) Categories
  - D) Labels

- **What does the "Archive" function do in Gmail?**

  - A) Permanently deletes an email
  - B) Saves an email to a designated folder
  - C) Removes an email from the inbox without deleting it
  - D) Marks an email as spam

- **Which Gmail feature allows you to undo sending an email?**

  - A) Recall Email
  - B) Delay Send
  - C) Undo Send
  - D) Retract Email

- **How can you access Gmail offline?**

  - A) Enable "Offline Mode" in Gmail settings
  - B) Download the Gmail mobile app
  - C) Use a third-party email client
  - D) Use the "Download Emails" feature

- **What is the primary purpose of the "Spam" folder in Gmail?**

  - A) To store important emails

- B) To store deleted emails
- C) To store unsolicited and potentially harmful emails
- D) To store archived emails

- **Which Gmail feature helps you prioritize important emails?**

  - A) Starred
  - B) Priority Inbox
  - C) Filters
  - D) Labels

- **What is Google Chat in Gmail used for?**

  - A) Sending large files
  - B) Instant messaging and collaboration
  - C) Video conferencing
  - D) Scheduling emails

- **Who is known as the "Father of Computers"?**

  - A) Alan Turing
  - B) Charles Babbage
  - C) John von Neumann
  - D) Steve Jobs

- **What was the name of the first mechanical computer designed by Charles Babbage?**

  - A) Analytical Engine
  - B) Difference Engine
  - C) ENIAC
  - D) Colossus

- **Which of the following was the first general-purpose electronic digital computer?**

  - A) UNIVAC
  - B) ENIAC
  - C) EDVAC
  - D) IBM 701

- **Who is credited with writing the first algorithm intended to be processed by a machine?**

  - A) Ada Lovelace
  - B) Grace Hopper
  - C) Alan Turing
  - D) John McCarthy

- **What was the first commercially successful personal computer?**

- A) Apple II
- B) IBM PC
- C) Commodore 64
- D) Altair 8800

- Which programming language, developed in the 1950s, is considered one of the oldest high-level programming languages?

  - A) C++
  - B) Java
  - C) FORTRAN
  - D) Python

- Who developed the World Wide Web?

  - A) Vinton Cerf
  - B) Bill Gates
  - C) Tim Berners-Lee
  - D) Steve Jobs

- What was the primary purpose of the ARPANET, the precursor to the modern internet?

  - A) Military communication
  - B) Academic research
  - C) Commercial use
  - D) Public social networking

- What does "IBM" stand for?

  - A) International Business Machines
  - B) Internet Business Machines
  - C) Independent Business Machines
  - D) Integrated Business Machines

- Which computer was used in the Apollo missions to navigate and land on the moon?

  - A) IBM System/360
  - B) UNIVAC I
  - C) ENIAC
  - D) Apollo Guidance Computer

- Which technology was used in the first generation of computers?

  - A) Transistors
  - B) Integrated Circuits
  - C) Vacuum Tubes
  - D) Microprocessors

- **What is the main characteristic of second-generation computers?**

  - A) Use of transistors
  - B) Use of vacuum tubes
  - C) Use of microprocessors
  - D) Use of artificial intelligence

- **Which of the following is an example of a first-generation computer?**

  - A) IBM 1401
  - B) UNIVAC I
  - C) PDP-8
  - D) Cray-1

- **Which technology marked the beginning of the third generation of computers?**

  - A) Vacuum Tubes
  - B) Transistors
  - C) Integrated Circuits
  - D) Microprocessors

- **What is the main feature of fourth-generation computers?**

  - A) Use of vacuum tubes
  - B) Use of transistors
  - C) Use of integrated circuits
  - D) Use of microprocessors

- **Which generation of computers is characterized by the use of artificial intelligence?**

  - A) First generation
  - B) Second generation
  - C) Fourth generation
  - D) Fifth generation

- **Which of the following was a key development in the second generation of computers?**

  - A) Introduction of magnetic core memory
  - B) Development of integrated circuits
  - C) Creation of the microprocessor
  - D) Use of machine language

- **What was the primary storage medium for first-generation computers?**

  - A) Magnetic disks
  - B) Punch cards
  - C) Magnetic tapes

- D) Solid-state drives

- **Which generation of computers saw the introduction of the graphical user interface (GUI)?**

    - A) First generation
    - B) Second generation
    - C) Third generation
    - D) Fourth generation

- **What distinguishes fifth-generation computers from earlier generations?**

    - A) Use of vacuum tubes
    - B) Advanced parallel processing and artificial intelligence
    - C) Use of transistors
    - D) Use of integrated circuits

Top of Form
Bottom of Form

"The future belongs to those who believe in the beauty of their dreams"
"Eleanor Roosevelt"
"Success is not the key to happiness. Happiness is the key to success.
If you love what you are doing, you will be successful".
"Albert Schweitzer"
"The only way to do great work is to love what you do.
"Steve Jobs"
"Don't watch the clock; do what it does. Keep going"
"Sam Levenson"
"The harder you work for something, the
greater you'll feel when you achieve it."

Ward No-17, Basatpur Dighwara Saran Bihar-841207

www.ingramcontent.com/pod-product-compliance
Lightning Source LLC
Chambersburg PA
CBHW080435240526
45479CB00015B/1181